PENGUIN BOOKS

HORSES OF THE CAMARGUE

Hans Silvester, born in the Black Forest of Germany, has been living in a small French village of Provence, near Gordes, since 1962. His numerous studies of social conditions, especially in the Middle East and South America, did much to establish his reputation as an adept and concerned reporter. He has published several books, notably one on the Camargue (with Jean Giono) and *Tsiganes et Gitans* (with Jean-Paul Clébert), a portrait of the gypsies of Europe and South America. His most recent book, *Petanque et Jeu Provençal,* was published in France in 1976. He recently lived in Spain, where he worked for the magazine *Geo,* and he is now at work on two projects, a book about Les Maures, in the south of France, and a portfolio of color photographs of scarecrows.

World-esteemed zoologist Konrad Lorenz is a member of the American Academy of Arts and Sciences, among other distinguished associations, the recipient of many prestigious awards, and the author of a number of books, including *On Aggression* and *Evolution and Modification of Behavior.* His theory that an animal's behavior is a result of adaptive evolution became the basis of a major school of thought.

photographs and text
by Hans Silvester

Horses of the Camargue

Preface by Konrad Lorenz

PENGUIN BOOKS

Penguin Books Ltd, Harmondsworth,
Middlesex, England
Penguin Books, 625 Madison Avenue,
New York, New York 10022, U.S.A.
Penguin Books Australia Ltd, Ringwood,
Victoria, Australia
Penguin Books Canada Limited, 2801 John Street,
Markham, Ontario, Canada L3R 1B4
Penguin Books (N.Z.) Ltd, 182–190 Wairau Road,
Auckland 10, New Zealand

First published in France under the title *Chevaux de Camargue* by
Editions du Chêne 1975
First published in the United States of America by
The Viking Press (A Studio Book) 1976
Published in Penguin Books 1979

LIBRARY OF CONGRESS CATALOGING IN PUBLICATION DATA
Silvester, Hans Walter.
    Horses of the Camargue.
    Translation of Chevaux de Camargue.
    1. Camargue horse—Pictorial works. 2. Horses—
France—Camargue, Ile de la—Pictorial works.
3. Camargue, Ile de la—Description and travel—Views.
I. Title.
SF293.c28s5713   1979   779'.32   79-14744
ISBN 0 14 00.5360 3

Printed in Switzerland by Imprimerie Attinger, Neuchâtel
Set in Times Roman

Translated by Jill Hugh-Jones

All the photographs were taken with Leica and Leicaflex cameras
and different Leitz lenses varying from 28 to 400 mm.

Recently I have seen several beautiful books of photographs, for many of today's photographers bring an artist's understanding to the portrayal of nature. Only a few among them have undertaken to depict a landscape in all its living beauty. Hans Silvester has done so admirably. His pictures of the Camargue convey to the reader, whether he has ever been there or not, a love of nature in all its manifestations—the delicate filigree of ice-crystals around a reed in a frozen pond, the monumental strength of fighting stallions—and reveal an inherent sense of beauty more typical of the painter than of the photographer.

The purpose of a book like this is twofold: first, to give the jaded urban-dweller the opportunity to experience at first hand the beauty of the Camargue or a similar area, and secondly to appeal to the public to call a halt to the destruction of the few remaining virgin landscapes in Europe, with their irreplaceable riches. Hans Silvester's book achieves both these aims. May it succeed in inspiring those who see it.

Konrad Lorenz

Introduction

The men who painted horses and bulls on the cave walls at Lascaux, 17,000 years ago, were making one of the most significant gestures in human history, little though they were aware of it. What they intended to make was a powerful charm to call up the prey they hunted. To us, the paintings show the start of a process that has been going on for thousands of years: the taming and training of the beasts of the wild.

Among all the animals that came gradually to accept man's dominion, the horse takes pride of place. When man set about mastering the world he lived in, the horse was his friend and partner. Whether galloping into battle, or only to the chase—whether pushing off into the unknown to search for pastures new, or pulling the plough that broke them for man's use—wherever men went, his horse went too.

It seems likely that the wild horse as a distinct species has died out completely. There is some evidence, it is true, of the survival of wild horses in Russia, on the borders of Outer Mongolia. But whether these are true wild horses, or the result of cross-breeding with the domestic horses, it is impossible to say. What we can say for sure is that the wild horses of the Camargue are not really 'wild', either in species or character. They know man, and are not afraid of him; but because they live in the wild the whole year round they often go for weeks at a time without setting eyes on a human being. They fend for themselves on the natural pastures where they roam, only very occasionally eating fodder brought along for them by man. They never see the inside of a stable.

There are three kinds of herds roaming the Camargue: family herds, made up of stallions, mares, and foals; young herds of two- to four-year-olds; and—during the winter when they are not being used for riding—herds of saddle-horses, which live in great fenced pastures and move around according to the season.

As all the land suitable for cultivation is given over to the vine, or to rice or asparagus, the only terrain left for the horses is marshland. The mares, left entirely to their biological function of reproduction, hardly meet any human beings. Consequently they are extremely wary and shy off at any attempt to approach or touch them.

There are striking differences, of course, between one herd and the next, depending on the amount of contact between the herd and its owner or his herdsmen. Some of the herds are still very wild indeed. My purpose was to watch and photograph the horses of the Camargue, and I particularly wanted to capture the everyday life and behaviour of one of the herds.

The way a particular horse in a given herd behaves is a highly individual thing (this is especially true of the stallions), and so one cannot generalize from a single observation. A horse's reactions will be different, obviously, if an outsider is present. If an intruder gets among the herd, all heads turn to look at him, and though they will after a while settle down again to their grazing, the horses will still be on the alert, conscious of the alien presence.

Before you can hope to be truly accepted by the horses—mingling with them and disturbing them as little as a hare or a rabbit in the grass—you have to be with them over a long period, and for long stretches at a time.

For my plan to work, this kind of acceptance was crucial. I spent weeks and weeks over my novitiate, living among the horses day and night, to give them every chance of getting used to me. At last, my presence came to be taken for granted. But without this regular preliminary contact, which the horses came to regard as 'natural', my plan would never have had a chance.

Simply to get the horses accustomed to the smell and the sight of me was not enough. They had moved from uneasiness to indifference; to get them to know me properly, I fell back on the mysterious, Orphic power of the human voice. And it was this that won them round. Eventually, if I were to walk up to a herd that knew me, and start speaking to them as I came, they would stay where they were, unalarmed. If I did not speak, they would come up to me to make quite sure it was really me, and even in the dark I could soothe away any alarm by talking to them in a quiet, even voice.

This was the only form of contact I used. I never tried to stroke them or get too close, or even to stare at them too directly, for it made them uneasy. I just stayed still, and when I moved, moved slowly. I sat for hours in one spot, simply looking and waiting. After a time, one or two of the horses would come up and sniff me—which had its hazards on occasion. One day, for instance, a little foal came across and nosed me. For some reason it suddenly took fright and whinnied for its mother, and I found myself having to deal with a truculent mamma. In awkward situations such as that, the best thing you can do is again just talk—gently and reassuringly. If necessary, a shout will frighten them off. There were occasions, however, when a speedy withdrawal was called for.

The behaviour of domesticated animals is less, not more, predictable than that of wild animals. Even if they are used to living in semi-liberty, they are not strictly primitive in their responses, for these have been modified by cross-breeding and other forms of human interference.

Contrary to general belief, a horse can express a great deal by means of its features, especially its ears. Long experience has taught man to read these indicators, the barometer of the animal's moods. With time, one or two of the younger stallions would try to play with me, but the difference in strength between us made it very difficult. The bite of a playful young two-year-old is painful enough, and can leave quite a scar—but what about the slightly bigger ones, who have reached sexual maturity and whose reactions it is quite impossible to predict?

If you live with a herd of horses regularly, you run a good many more risks than if you merely visit it from time to time. You have to be extremely circumspect, and never forget that a stallion may see a man in the vicinity of his mares for some days without objecting, and then quite suddenly turn jealous and attack. Or he may attack in order to protect them. His instinct is to keep his harem together. If one of the mares leaves the group to go and investigate you, he may turn vicious.

Very few of the photographs were taken on horseback, as a rider will intrigue the herd even more than a man on foot. Stallions resent the presence of a strange horse with or without a rider, and prepare to attack the minute they see one approach.

To take these photographs, I spent from three to six months in the year in the Camargue over a period of five years. It was only through the kindness and co-operation of the owners of the herds and their staff that I was able to take them at all. Without their assistance, this book could never have been written.

The Camargue

North of Arles, the Rhône divides, and its twin streams flow to the sea across a broad, alluvial plain.

There is always something eerie about a delta. The river has lost its momentum; its current slows and moves sluggishly (23). Then the estuary opens, and there is the clash of opposing forces as the sea flings itself against the crawling stream. Insidiously the river counter-attacks, pushing its muddy coils into the bright waves. Flotsam borne along by one is carried off by the other, to be tossed back again. The earth, too, is unstable, disputed by river and sea. Here the current lays down mud that will wash away in the next rainstorm; there, dunes are moulded one day and swept flat by the mistral the next.

For centuries fresh water, salt water, and earth have intermingled and blended, constantly altering the face of the landscape (2). One's surroundings can be completely transformed in the space of a lifetime—though this is less true now than it used to be, since the construction of the Rhône barrages and the drainage canals, which have brought the wayward river under control, improvements which have in fact themselves contributed to the changing nature of the scenery.

Once, the Rhône hereabouts branched into a whole network of streams which threaded their way erratically through the delta, always nosing out new courses. Now it has only two, firmly disciplined by dykes. The heart of the Camargue is the Etang de Vaccarès, a vast lagoon dotted with islets and fringed with peninsulas. Strangely enough, this huge stretch of water, over 17,000 acres of it, is hardly anywhere more than three feet deep.

The Vaccarès contains a cluster of wooded islands known as the Bois des Rièges. These lakeland woods are very old indeed. They consist of dense, almost impenetrable, thickets of juniper. The Vaccarès, together with most of its banks, now forms part of the Camargue Nature Reserve. The lake is the haunt of flamingoes, which nest in colonies on one of the small islands. You can see great throngs of them, dabbling for food in the shallow waters.

In the brilliant sunshine of high summer, mirages shimmer on the air, making shining pools and ponds upon perfectly dry ground. It becomes impossible to judge distances.

West of the Petit Rhône is an area of small lakes and sand-dunes covered in pine scrub—marvellous umbrella pines with a ground-cover of rosemary (9). The north of the Camargue is a district of vineyards, rice fields, and orchards. The farms, known as *mas*, are biggish for the region—250 acres or more. Sheep are grazed on the dry pastures, and bulls and horses reared in the marshier parts. But arable holdings are more economic nowadays than stock-breeding, so horses and bulls are gradually losing out to crops. The only town of any size in the Camargue is Les Saintes-Maries-de-la-Mer, once a little fishing village, now a tourist resort. Here, everybody knows everybody. The locals meet in the various cafés every evening to swap the latest news over a glass of pastis. Here you will hear of such-and-such a horse being for sale; or that there's just been an accident; or that so-and-so has walked out on so-and-so. The day's bag or catch will be discussed, and the latest bull-fight re-fought. The atmosphere is unlike anywhere else, and to the outsider, unfamiliar with the Camargue and the Camarguais, the talk is hard to follow. There are still fishermen in the town who make a living by catching eel in the lakes or *tellines* (small shellfish) on the seashore.

At the end of May thousands of gypsies flock to Les Saintes-Maries-de-la-Mer for the annual festival in honour of their patron saint, St Sarah.

Horizon—Dark and Light

Unbroken and flawlessly straight, the horizon divides the Camargue into two distinct worlds: earth and water beneath, air and sky overhead. On a windless day the horizon will dissolve into space and vanish, confounding earth and heaven, and the glassy water becomes the sky reversed. Across the marsh flamingoes stoop to meet their reflections. Flights of birds, skimming the sky, skim the water as well. A horse looks down at his own face. The sun smiles back at the sun—its light, glancing off the polished water, never reaches the dim world lying beneath. A horse splashing softly along sends circles rippling from his hooves to die a double death—on the surface, and again in shadow on the mud.

It is not a silent world. Listening, you hear a host of small noises, near and far. Where do they come from? It could be anywhere in this sunny limbo, neither earth nor sky. The horizon's line divides, but the miracle of light constantly restores to this world its underlying unity.

The sun sets twice: in the sky, and in the shining water where it sinks to rest. The Camargue loses its daylight blue and for a moment all is gold. Then gold gives way to flame, and the sky melts into its reflection. The evening deepens swiftly into violet. Over in the east it is already dark; westward the sky is still streaked with sunset colour, long after the sun has set.

Suddenly, the mantle of the dark is pierced by stars. Night has come, but not black dark: a luminous dark, in which you can see, and yet see nothing.

Now land and water alike wake to a murmurous activity unknown in daylight. Hundreds of small wild creatures are going about their business. Only man, a diurnal animal, flinches at the dark. It bothers him, and so do these rustlings all around he cannot account for.

The Horses

Very little is known about the ancestors and origins of the horses of the Camargue. But we can say one thing: the horses in the cave paintings at Niaux and Lascaux (15,000 BC) are remarkably similar to their present-day counterparts in the Camargue.

It might well be that the wild horse that is known to have inhabited south-eastern France—the Solutré or Prjevalski horse—was the ancestor of the Camargue horse. If that is so, then the Camargue horse is near kin to the wild horse of Mongolia. The Camargue region, so wild and so difficult of access, may perhaps have offered a few semi-domesticated herds the seclusion enabling them to survive for century after century in almost unbroken liberty.

Ever since he began to tame horses, man has also taken a hand in the development of the breeds; but the Camargue horse—the 'primitive' horse, as it is called—has been tampered with less than most. It is a fairly small breed (13 or 14 hands at the most), sturdily built and rather square in the head. The foals are black or dark brown at birth, but then their coats turn grey, and by the age of four or five this fades to the characteristic white. The Camargue horse matures rather late and is considered full-grown at about five years old. But they live to a good age, often over twenty, and sometimes even to thirty. And they make good saddle-horses, even when quite old. A good brood mare will produce up to twenty foals in her lifetime.

Early records show there were 4,000 mares in the delta in the year 1550. Today they number around 750, but the number is increasing.

In 1968 the Camargue horse was officially recognized by the French National Stud as a separate breed. A selection of the best stud-horses takes place every year at Arles, under the patronage of the Nîmes National Stud. There are pronounced differences between the types of horse reared by the various stud-farms. A connoisseur can tell at a glance where a particular horse was bred. There have been many attempts to introduce new blood, mainly by cross-breeding with Barbs, Arabs, and Portuguese or Spanish horses. Until quite recently, breeding was practised chiefly with the aim of producing good working horses for use among the herds of bulls. Here the Camargue horse, ridden by skilled herdsmen, really comes into his own. Tough, quick to wheel and halt, surefooted even on slippery ground, ready to gallop even when up to his girths in water, he shows all the qualities needed for this exacting work. However, only a limited number of horses could be used for such work and so breeding unfortunately became uneconomic, and all too many horses ended up in the abattoirs—mostly mares. Nobody in the Camargue will ride a mare.

Today, fortunately, things are changing slightly, owing to the influx of tourists into the region and the increasing interest in riding shown by people from the nearby towns. Stud-owners in the Camargue have formed themselves into an association. The bigger stud-farms own about a hundred mares, but the average is more like fifteen to twenty-five. Each breeder has his own brand to enable his animals to be identified (*right*, some examples).

In the Camargue the herds fend for themselves, and as the natural vegetation is not of the richest, each herd requires something between five to fifteen acres of land per head in order to find adequate grazing. This pressure on the land helps to explain the small number of herds to be found in the region.

Spring

The horses of the Camargue, like lovers, love the spring. At this time of year the herd is frisky and full of life. The weather is warm, but not yet hot enough to bring out the swarms of biting insects that torment the poor animals later in the year (1). Fodder is plentiful and varied, with new tufts of rushes, tender new grass and leaves, and the water full of juicy weeds.

The horses roll over on the ground and rub against the trees or against each other, shedding their winter coats in handfuls. The birds fly in from Africa: bee-eaters and swallows, rollers and hoopoes, joining the nightingales and cuckoos already here. Nests are everywhere. The whole world cheeps. A duck bustles across the water out of the way of a horse, her string of ducklings trickling in her wake. The pools are covered in starry white water-crowfoot (10). For the horses, as for every other living thing, spring is the season for love: both for mating and for giving birth. Stallions fight furiously, and all around you can hear the neighing and whinnying of horses exulting in life and the urge to renew life. Mares in foal cluster together and nibble each other affectionately (11), while the fiery stallion, their lord and master, guards them jealously (31). The new foals, in their plushy coats of chestnut and black, show up warmly against the pale coats of the herd (29).

Egrets

There is no forest proper in the Camargue, but the scrub woodland of umbrella pine forms a close canopy to ward off the rays of the sun and afford good cover for bird-life. In these pine thickets, colonies of little egrets come to nest.

Hundreds of couples are bringing up families together. You can sometimes count twenty nests or more in a single tree. From a good way off, you can see flashes of white against the leaves. Then you hear the crying and squawking of the baby egrets announcing their hunger. Nothing ever satisfies them, though the parent birds shuttle back and forth most busily, disgorging the frogs and fish they have swallowed to fill their ever-ravenous young.

An unbelievable clamour rises from the nests. Fledglings squabble over their food; the slightly bigger ones sit unsteadily on the branches and in their greed try to flap off to greet their parents' return, which sometimes ends in disaster: if they tumble out of the tree, dusk will almost certainly bring along a hungry fox to make his supper off them. As soon as the young can fly, the colony disperses, and peace returns to the pines.

Until our own day, man's exploitation and destruction of the natural world was a more or less unconscious process: man made use of what he needed, and threw away his waste for nature to deal with. But the human population of the earth has been increasing disproportionately fast lately. Clear water and clean air have become a rarity. Much of what we eat is artificial. The balance of nature is much more precise and delicate than we like to believe—or indeed than we are capable of grasping as we grow gradually out of touch with the way nature works. And today our continued senseless assault on the natural environment has put our own survival at risk.

In these photographs of the Camargue you can see a countryside which is even today virtually unknown—at least, those parts of it which have been protected by their extreme isolation. Not very long ago it would have been possible to preserve the whole of the Camargue in all its wild charm, instead of just a few privileged areas. But here, as elsewhere, the demands of modern life and the short-sighted interests of individuals or groups have combined against the helpless wild.

Wild Life

The immense marshy pastures of the Camargue support a rich variety of wild life. There are dozens of species of birds, of course. Apart from flamingoes (3), the marshes and reedy lagoons contain purple heron (41), grey heron, little egret (44), cattle egret (6 & 7), black-backed heron, plover and bittern.

The marshy terrain also attracts the smaller waders and water-birds. There are stilt (46), avocet, oystercatcher, coot, moorhen, and water-rail; cormorants and many different kinds of ducks, of which the commonest is the mallard and the least common, the sheldrake. Flocks of gulls frequent the shore (48) and can often be seen flying further inland; while tern and blackheaded gulls form large nesting colonies.

Then there are birds of prey: buzzards (49), kites, Bonelli's eagle, kestrels, goshawks, long-eared owl and screech-owl. Cuckoos and jays are common, as are jackdaws and crows. There are partridge and pheasant among the game-birds, and among the smaller species, nightingales, tits and linnets. Some of the less common birds are worth special mention because of their lovely plumage: the kingfisher, the roller, the bee-eater (45), the hoopoe with his elegant crest (47), the oriole, and the gay little goldfinch. No other region in France—a country with over 400 different species—can boast such a concentration of birds, either in sheer numbers or diversity of species.

Wild animals, on the other hand, are not nearly so numerous, though there are rabbits, hares, badgers, foxes, wild boar, coypu, marten, polecats, weasels and squirrels. Otter and the European beaver are extremely rare. Among the reptiles are green lizards, turtles, frogs, tree-frogs, and various snakes.

The herds of horses and bulls make their distinct contribution to the balance of nature in the Camargue. For one thing, without them, the lakes and ponds would very soon be choked with weed (43).

Many of the birds in the Camargue are ground-nesting species; and it is a remarkable fact that the nests are scarcely ever harmed by either bulls or horses. Usually, if they come across a nest while browsing, they will walk round it, the mother bird protesting noisily at the intrusion. The horses are perfectly at home with all the lesser animals of the region. Only two will frighten them: the wild boar, whose mere scent can arouse panic, and the snake—at least if it rears up suddenly in front of them.

Horses and Birds

The only birds impudent enough to use a horse's back as a perch are cattle egrets, magpies, jackdaws and starlings. The horses have no objection to egrets and starlings, but they do not at all care for the magpies' pecking and scratching. Magpies find a horse's back a useful vantage-point for spying out food in the surrounding pastures. The jackdaw actually feeds from the horse's back, pecking up insects (ticks mostly) out of the hair. However, in spring, the jackdaws steal tufts of horsehair for nesting material. To do this in spite of the horse's resistance needs cunning: one jackdaw pulls the horse's mane while another pecks out some hair. The horse of course tosses his head and tries to shrug them off, but the wily birds simply take wing and hover for a while before returning to the attack (5). Three or four jackdaws will collect on one horse's back to 'work it over' before going on to the next. Sometimes half-a-dozen birds can unsettle an entire herd by bothering them in this way.

The relations between horses and cattle egrets are more cordial. When the horses graze among the reedbeds, they move leisurely along through the shallows, startling a host of little creatures—frogs, fishes, snakes—who dart away in terror. The vigilant egrets, standing sentinel on the horses' heads, swoop on them at once (6). Erect on high, they survey the marsh around, and as soon as suitable prey comes into view they pounce on it. Then they fly back to their perch.

If there happen to be more egrets looking for a perch than horses to provide one, there will be a free-for-all. You very rarely see an egret consenting to share his accommodation with another (7).

During the day, if the horse he is perching on happens to lie down for a nap, the egret stays at his post, dozing or preening his feathers. The counter-benefits he renders his host are considerable. Splashing so often through water, the horse gets his legs plastered with leeches; these are quickly picked off by the egret. The same is true of stinging insects—in particular the horsefly, which attacks the animal's belly.

Horses and egrets live on terms of mutual trust. In spring the foals tease the birds, making them fly up and then chasing them; but the birds know quite well they are only playing. The bond between horse and egret is so close that if one is alarmed his companion immediately senses it, to the benefit of their mutual security. There are four other species of bird that live on neighbourly terms with the horses: the swallow, wagtail, lark, and hoopoe. The wagtail and hoopoe hop fearlessly round the horse's hooves looking for food. The swallow will almost brush the horse's back as it dips after gnats, and sometimes even swoops under its belly.

Birth

April is the month when the foals are born, after a gestation of eleven months. The mares nearly always foal at night: it is quite rare for a foal to be born in daylight.

The sun has gone down. A mare, sensing that her time has come, leaves the herd. The stallion does not interfere. Head down, she seems to be inspecting the terrain—a low hummock, protected by a few bushes, seems to engage her attention. She circles it once or twice, and then walks calmly back to the herd.

Some hours later, when the horses are grazing quietly in the darkness, the mare leaves them once again and makes for the spot she has chosen. She lies down on her side, her head on the ground. Her flanks heave and contract, and after a while the muzzle and forelegs of the foal emerge: a terrific straining effort—and the head appears (12). The mare gets on to her feet, staggers a step or two, lies down again. As soon as its forequarters are free, the foal begins to move its legs about and shake its head. One more effort on the mare's part, and the rest of her foal is born, still swathed in the sac, out of which it struggles to get free (13, 14). Its little hooves are quite soft, but harden as they dry in the air. Now the mare takes a few minutes' rest, while her baby tries to scramble on to its feet. The mare gets up and looks at what she has produced. Then she nudges and noses him upright, for he must begin to suck straightaway, and he can only do this standing up (14). She does not lick him exactly: the air will soon dry out his coat for him. After a few fruitless attempts, the foal manages to clamber on to his wobbly, spindly legs. He sways about for a minute, and then quickly finds his balance and gives a little whinny of triumph. The mare goes on nuzzling softly at his damp body, and a few minutes later, evacuates the afterbirth. Scarcely an hour has gone by from the time the mare left the herd to the moment her foal managed to stand on his feet. Suddenly, as if at a signal, they are rejoined by the herd, which closes in round them. Several horses, including the stallion, survey the new arrival, snuffing at it. The mare makes no objection. However, the interest shown by the herd is very short-lived, and mother and son are left to themselves again. The foal is hungry, but it takes him several clumsy attempts to find his mother's teats and begin to suck. Still, there he is, only an hour and a half after his first appearance, sucking away greedily and successfully. The first milk, the colostrum, contains antibodies essential for the foal's survival. It is at this point that the mare-foal relationship seems to take shape. From now on the mare is extremely protective, and no longer allows the other horses near her foal. In other words, the maternal instinct is manifested only when the foal begins to nurse, not actually at birth. Once he has taken some nourishment, the new foal is strong enough to follow the herd. His first day, though, is almost entirely given over to sucking and sleeping, while his mother grazes close by him.

From the second day he falls in with the normal rhythm of the herd: he follows his mother, frolics with the other foals, and gradually learns to nibble grass (17–20).

The Foals

Like all baby creatures, foals are very inquisitive and eager to explore their new world. They begin to nibble grasses and sedges, learning to distinguish the various kinds by taste, though their chief food is their mothers' milk.

They play together, sometimes as many as a dozen of them at a time, gambolling and galloping about all over the place (19, 20). I have seen a foal put up a hare and go streaking after it for sheer love of a gallop. The mares like to feel that their foals are under their eye and grow agitated if they move too far off; but foals turn a deaf ear to maternal whinnyings—though if one of them calls to his mother, she will arrive at the trot. A hungry foal will go unhesitatingly to the nearest mare. But he will be brusquely repulsed—only his own mother will let him suck. If this happens, the frightened foal snaps his jaws together once or twice as a sign of submission, and this saves him a scolding, as all the mares will turn around to see what is wrong and his own mother will come to the rescue. The mares of the Camargue are most loving towards their foals, and the foals respond with playful caresses, such as rubbing their heads against their mothers (16). But they are happiest when playing with one another. When tired they lie down in a bunch on the grass and go to sleep. If a foal feels hungry and finds his mother asleep, he wakes her up.

The foals' activity depends on the sort of terrain the herd is covering at any given time. If it is grazing the marsh (17) or the lagoons, the going is quite hard for the little ones, especially if they have to follow the herd through water (23); and as soon as they reach dry ground they will fold up their legs and lie down at once to sleep (21, 22). If a particular stretch of marsh is actually dangerous, one of the mares stands guard over the foals while the other mares feed; surrounded by foals, she waits there like a patient nanny till the others have eaten their fill (18). Sometimes another mare will come up to relieve her. Apart from sniffing at them now and then, the father of the foals takes no notice of his offspring at all.

Although a mare will always defend her foal if need arise, her more usual recourse is to gallop out of danger with her foal close to her side (15). She only resorts to kicking or biting to protect him during the very first few days of his life.

For a young foal, life in the Camargue is full of risk. To begin with, the soft terrain of the marshes makes it hard for him, with his small hooves, to keep his footing. He gets leg-weary, and may then collapse with exhaustion and drown. Trodden or broken reed-stems may get into his hooves and set up an inflammation. If the herd panics for some reason, the foals may easily get kicked. This can also happen to a foal whose mother's milk has run dry if he goes up to one of the other mares to be suckled.

Day and Night

The pattern of a horse's life here is not split by the rigid alternation of day and night. For the herd, night does not necessarily mean sleep. I had the opportunity of observing one herd throughout May and June. The horses would go on grazing after the sun had gone down till as late as eleven o'clock. They would then close ranks gradually and stand for a time without moving; after which they would lie down, one after another, the stallion as well, and go to sleep. Except for a few horses who slept on their feet so as to be ready to wake and move at the least alarm, the herd slept lying down, some of them snoring loudly. Two hours later, they got up again and began to browse. At about three in the morning they lay down for another sleep, and this went on until the first flush of light coloured the horizon. Sometimes the stallion would wake the herd with his neighing.

The foals' regular rhythm of feeding, sleeping, and playing went on just the same whether it was day or night. The mares in foal hardly lay down at all, but would sleep on their feet most of the time, perhaps because of the movements they felt within their womb. If, being weary, they fell into a deeper sleep for a minute, they would lose their balance, totter sideways, and just manage to save themselves from falling. Horses, of course, have far better night vision than men, as well as a keener sense of hearing and smell. The awareness of their surroundings this gives them is almost uncanny.

Horses are creatures of habit. They like familiar, well-worn tracks. They obey an inner rhythm which gives rise, day and night, to a regular pattern of activity: grazing, going down to water, sleeping or playing about; and they do not readily allow this pattern to be interrupted. Exactly how an animal's inherited instinct works is still obscure. All we know is that a horse's perception of the thousand elements that make up its environment is infinitely more sensitive than ours. In thick darkness horses will find their way without the least difficulty. Anything new or different in their path awakens their suspicion.

If anything should arise to interfere with their three dominant senses of sight, hearing and smell—high winds, for instance, in the case of hearing, or an overpowering smell—they become wary at once.

Summer

Summer in the Camargue: brooding heat, rare patches of shade, the pools dried up, the earth cracked and hard, the blue days endless. No rain for months on end, and what water there is in the ponds is slimy and stagnant in the blazing sun (38). The earth is powdery; the fresh green of grass and reeds has yellowed.

The horses laze and slumber till dusk, when they revive a little. For hours on end they stay in one spot, on a ridge or a rise if they can find one, where there is some chance of a slight ruffle of breeze. They stand in a close circle, their heads to the middle, all their tails ceaselessly on the move to flog off horseflies and mosquitoes, doggedly living out the sweltering hours; while above their heads great dragonflies float on humming wings to snap a stray mosquito. If they can, the horses move into a patch of shade, but shade is scarce in this bald wilderness. The foals are growing up fast and are almost weaned. Now they are feeding normally on grass and reeds, and are less mischievous and more experienced; the mares leave them more to themselves.

The horses love the succulent water-plants in the ponds and lagoons and wade into the water right up to their eyes to get at them (23). The worst hardship summer brings is the lack of water. Most of the familiar drinking-places go dry or brackish in the heat, and clean water is hard to come by in spite of the frequent storms, which are very heavy at this time of year and terrify the horses.

The Stallion

The horse-breeders (rather than natural selection) pick out the stallion they intend to breed from and leave him to run with the herd of mares for two or three months. This selection is the one deliberate piece of human interference in the life of the herd. The chosen stallion becomes the leader of the herd, and his rule over his mares is strict. He keeps them from straying out of the group, and stands guard over them (29, 30).

If one of his harem is wayward or rebellious he will make his displeasure felt—even bite her, on occasion, if she is obstinate. He is by no means a tender spouse. He rules by force, not affection. But he does not invariably have all his own way.

The fillies are rather shy and scared at their first contact with a male. It takes them some time to get used to the new situation (25, 26).

The mature ones may rebuff the stallion's advances before they come in season, not hesitating to use their hooves if necessary to ward him off, especially if they are suckling a foal and consequently in a nervous protective frame of mind.

But when in season, it is the mares themselves who make the first approach. The stallion will mount a mare in season several times over, day or night (27, 28). During May, in fact, the stallion has a most strenuous time. He is in a state of constant excitement, so engrossed with his harem he hardly finds time to eat and sleep. A stallion in charge of a herd needs—and clearly has—prodigious reserves of energy to meet the demands of the season.

Mares in season are very jealous and vie with one another for the favours of the male; in fact some can be so possessive that they quite definitely frustrate his moves in the direction of other mares. It also happens, on the other hand, that a contrary mare will refuse the stallion alto-gether—or, indeed, the other way round.

The stallion marks the bounds of his herd's grazing-grounds by the rank smell of his urine and dung, and reinforces his frontier by urinating at certain spots along it each time he passes that way. Before doing so he snuffs the air to discover if any strange stallion has trespassed into his sector. This is easy to recognize, as the latter would have urinated in the same spot. His nose can tell him straightaway if a mare in season or another stallion is anywhere in the neighbourhood; and a stallion of the Camargue will kick down fences and swim canals and lakes in order to come at a mare (24).

He is the brain of the herd. He takes the decisions for everyone in it. If the stallion is taken away, the mares are confused and at a loss for some time, until one of them eventually takes the lead.

The Herd of Young Stallions

Among wild horses, it used to be the leader of the herd who expelled the young stallions from the herd. Today, in the Camargue, it is man who removes them.

These young males form a separate group where they can learn how to behave and how to fight. They struggle for predominance, but they are so quarrelsome that none of them remains master for long. Nearly every day they indulge in brief mock-battles with one another, striving to get the upper hand. But no-one wins or loses. It is all in play.

The game begins almost invariably with two young horses sniffing a pile of dung. They then start to paw the ground, squeal, and try to sniff at each other's genitals. Each resists; so then they turn in their tracks (59); stop short; kneel down, and try to bite each other's forelegs. Then they get to their feet again and rear up face to face, hooves in the air, trying to overawe their rival (60). They drop hooves, and then again rear up. This goes on over and over again, getting more violent each time, but although they bite at each other quite fiercely, neither gets hurt; it is a fight without malice. These battles can last some time, often until a third stallion intervenes or until one of the pair gets tired of the kicking and biting and moves off.

This mock-fighting is the young stallion's apprentice-ship. In a truly wild state it would prepare him for the stage in the life of the herd when he has to fight it out with his rivals for possession of the mares. But in the Camargue the breeder intervenes, selecting the stud horse and cas-trating the rest.

The Duel

The herd is browsing peacefully—the foals frisking about, the stallion feeding, as usual, a little way apart from his mares. All of a sudden, he lifts his head and breathes the air, nostrils flaring. He gives a loud neigh. The mares close up; the foals run to their mothers; the whole group looks fixedly at their leader. He neighs again. Then he bucks violently, stops again to snuff the air, and begins to pluck and pound the earth with his forefeet. All point their heads to look in the same direction: from the horizon, a horse is bearing down upon them at full gallop. It is a stallion, who has scented the mares in season and come to do battle for them.

The leader of the herd gives wild leaps in the air and paws the ground with his hooves, gathering up his strength and bunching his powerful muscles (31, 32). The strange stallion comes surging towards him; he opens wide his jaws, bares his teeth (33), and plunges at the enemy. Breast to breast, they both rear up on their hind-legs (34). One, with another frantic bound, turns rightabout and bites; his enemy kicks backward. They are aiming at the genitals (35). The maddened pair resolves into a single mass of furious flesh and muscle, twisting and leaping. They rear and kick, manes and tails whipping and threshing. They tear with their teeth at one another's flesh, and the air is loud with the clashing of jaws on air and the dull thud of hooves against solid flanks.

Legs and withers are laced with bleeding gashes, but the two warriors fight on, seeming to feel no pain. Stockstill, the mares and foals look on.

The stallions realize that they are equals in strength. They change tactics. Jaws snapping, they charge the watching herd of mares and foals at full gallop, and put them to flight. The panic-stricken mares are chased in one direction by one stallion, only to be driven back again by the other. Then they sweep along together in a frenzy of flying hooves—mares, foals, and stallions.

The stallions encounter each other in their pelting gallop, and the fight breaks out afresh. Terror-stricken mares and foals swerve away to escape them. The stallions break off and thunder in pursuit, galloping between the mares and splitting the group; the herd goes at full stretch again, ears back, heads out, tails streaming be-hind, like a pack in full cry, each stallion striving to divert as many mares as he can, to drive them off before him. This is the last stage of the duel. The leader of the herd has had four of his mares carried off, out of his harem of eighteen.

Autumn

In autumn the characteristic flora of the Camargue creates a rich backcloth for the ending of the year, the lilac-blue of sea-lavender and the golden brown of marsh samphire (52) setting off the bright yellow of tamarisk.

Flocks of migrants from the north stop here on their long journey south to Africa. What looks like millions of starlings swarm overhead in a black cloud, a most impressive sight. Hundreds of flamingoes pass over in v-formation, though many of these winter here in the Camargue. Thousands of duck come thronging from every corner of Europe. Often, the sombre shape of a cormorant is seen against the sky, and herons collect in groups to fish.

But autumn has its less agreeable visitors. Myriads of mosquitoes gather to torture men and beasts alike. They breed in millions at this season. Just before and just after sunset are the worst times, and the horses are the worst sufferers. They stamp and shake their heads and whisk their tails; rub against each other; even roll in the mud — but nothing avails for long against the whining hosts of tormentors. The invasion goes on for five or six weeks on average, depending on the weather. The first frosts put an end to it.

Mistral

Two days of uninterrupted rain. In the soft, featureless grey of the sky the clouds are quite effaced. This grey is very rare in Provence. The horses are damp and dejected, their coats sleeked and darkened by the wet. Tired of the incessant rain, heads lowered, ears and tails drooping, they stand and wait.

Suddenly, their heads come up. They turn their hind-quarters to the wind—and here the wind comes: the mistral, blowing down on them out of the north-west. It blows harder, sending the rain level with the ground to lash the horses' sides like fine needles, while the horses stand passive, their four feet planted firmly to resist the wind. At long last it clears. Blue gleams again in the sky to the north, and the last clouds go reeling seaward, flying before the wind. The stallion bellows and trots round his herd. The horses all roll on the damp ground to work off steam and warm themselves; then they begin to browse again (57). But the mistral rages on, tossing sheaves of spray across lagoons and ramming the breakers out at sea back upon themselves (54). It dries the sodden earth, flings up the sand, sends gust after gust swirling across the reedbeds and through the tamarisks. The sun drops abruptly out of the new-peeled sky; and now there is ice in the wind.

The horses make for shelter in the woods of the Petit-Rhône. They are by now once again in their thick winter coats, but one little fellow, the earliest of the new year's foals, seems frozen—he has only been in the world for three days and already he has learned of rain and wind. Like his elders, he turns his little rump to the wind. At intervals he runs to his mother to be comforted with milk.

During the night the temperature drops to freezing, but the morning sun soon warms things again, and the baby foal finds a sunny patch of grass to sleep on.

The mistral is said to keep to a rhythm: it blows for three, six, or nine days. If it goes on blowing for more than six days, it gets on the nerves of both humans and animals. After a week of it, the men say the relations between them and the bulls or horses in their charge show signs of strain.

By the same token, when the gale at last drops there is a general feeling of relief and gaiety: the horses gallop about; birds start to sing, frogs croak, and nature is herself again.

The Bulls

In the Lascaux cave-paintings, the bulls and horses, so beautifully observed and drawn by prehistoric man, are shown side by side. No doubt those Stone-Age bulls and horses grazed peacefully together just as the black bulls and white horses of the Camargue do today (66, 67).

The origins of this species of bull are doubtful, but it has been established that the bulls have been living here in the Rhône delta for thousands of years. A century back, the true Camargue breed was crossed with bulls from Spain, which resulted in a slightly heavier breed, without the characteristic lyre-shaped horns; the pure Camargue bull no longer exists.

The bulls of the Camargue are a good deal wilder than the horses. If approached, they run off at once, though if surprised and surrounded, or if they sense the threat of danger, they will charge without hesitation. Even the cows are dangerous, ready to use their horns in defence of their calves. But, owing to the age-long familiarity between bulls and horses (66), they will let a man in among them as long as he is on horseback. There are many more herds of bulls than there are of horses.

The bull of the Camargue is a smaller, lighter animal than the pure-bred Spanish bull. He is also faster, nimbler and more intelligent. His fodder and pasture-grounds are the same as the horses' and he, too, will wade into the water after sedges and weeds. He is more sensitive than the horse to rain and severe cold, and more susceptible to disease. Like horses, bulls indulge in fierce disputes for leadership. They don't usually get badly hurt, as the weaker bull is quick to cede victory.

Bull-breeding in the Camargue is directed to the production of good *cocardiers*—that is, bulls for the sport peculiar to Provence known as the *course libre*. The name *cocardier* comes from the red cockade tied to the bull's browband, which the *razetteurs* (young men, dressed by tradition in white) must pull off. To do this, they use only an iron hook, relying on their speed, agility, skill and perfect knowledge of the bull's reactions. Once in the ring, the *razetteur* runs up to the bull, and, stretching out his arm, tries to cut the string holding the cockade. If he is driven into a corner by the bull, he may jump over the barrier round the ring. The *razetteur* who succeeds in getting the cockade wins a money prize. It may happen that the bull, too, jumps the barrier in pursuit of his attacker—a situation keenly appreciated by the crowd and known as the *coup de la barrière*. It is dangerous, of course, for the *razetteur*. The spectators are enthralled by the bull's performance as much as by the man's, and applaud both parties impartially.

In the area enclosed by the triangle Marseilles–Avignon–Montpellier, the star bulls of the *course libre* are just as well known as the *razetteurs* themselves. Every town or village of any size has its bull-ring; and at every local festival the committee in charge will hire bulls for the occasion from local breeders—all of which adds to the breeders' income.

Some time before a *course libre* is due to start, the *gardians* or mounted herdsmen of the herd in question will ride off to select suitable bulls. These are led out of the herd and brought back, then taken away by lorry to the bull-ring. Afterwards they are brought back and again led out to pasture.

Winter

Although the Camargue is lapped by the Mediterranean, winters here can be severe. Every winter has its snowfall—usually light and fleeting, it is true; but some years the ponds and even the Vaccarès freeze hard enough for the horses to walk over the ice (70).

At the beginning of autumn, the horses begin to grow their thick winter coats, very necessary against the coming cold. It is the falling snow, rather than snow or ice on the ground, that bothers them (72). They scratch the snow away with their hooves to get at the grass (73), or move among the bushes to graze, where the ground is clear. During a hard frost, water can be hard to find. If the ice is thin, they put their hoof through to get at the water, but if it is too thick to crack, they will eat snow.

Some days the Camargue is shrouded in mist. The horses are quite unperturbed, their sharp ears and re-markable memory enabling them to find the right path even when it is lost to view (64).

Twigs and bark form a reserve food supply. If food really becomes scarce, the horses adapt themselves to hard times and make do with what they can find, until the return of spring gives them a chance to put on flesh again.

Very cold spells never last very long; but even so the water-birds can suffer badly, particularly the flamingoes. Those that over-winter here may have the misfortune to be caught by a sudden hard frost and, literally imprisoned by the ice, 'to lie in cold obstruction and to rot'.

Horses and Men

Young stallions of three to four years are caught on the marshes and taken to the stud-farm, where they are handled to get them used to being with people, before being mounted for the first time.

The initial stage of schooling is peculiar to the Camargue. One of the herdsmen, riding a very quiet horse, has the young horse, saddled, on a leading rein or rope. Once he has got used to the saddle and the first trainer, a second will mount him. The frightened horse begins, naturally, to rear and buck to get this strange weight off his back. He may try to roll on the ground to shed it, but the first man keeps him in check with the rope, while the presence of an experienced, well-mannered horse calms him down. Gradually he grows used to the situation, and after a few schooling sessions he is ready to be mounted normally. It is most important for the first rider to stay on. Otherwise the horse has won—and will try to repeat his victory every time a fresh attempt is made to mount him. Once schooled, the young stallion is usually castrated. In the Camargue no-one rides a mare.

The Camargue harness also has its local character. The Camargue saddle is said, and rightly, to be the most comfortable there is; padded fore and aft, with a rather high pommel and cantle, ending in a kind of backrest, it gives a very secure seat. The stirrups are shaped like a half-basket, so that it is impossible for the foot to be caught in them. In relation to the slight build of the horses, the harness is rather heavy and clumsy.

As the horses of the Camargue do not live in stables, the first job of the herdsman is of course to catch his horse. Armed with a *saquetoun* (bag of oats) he crosses the marsh towards it, calling softly. He slips a rope round its neck and leads it back to where he has left the tack. Then he saddles up, mounts, and rides off. These men have their own way of getting up; a sort of loose roll, or flop. When up, rider and horse move as one. They give the impression of being a single animal, not only in movement but also in mind. They trust one another—and, on dangerous ground, it is the horse who takes control.

The major part of the herdsmen's life is looking after the bulls. They have to guide the herds from pasture to pasture, ride in to fetch out the sick animals and so on. And for all necessary jobs, their one tool is the trident—which has become the symbol of the Camargue.

Branding the young bullocks is the excuse for a special fête, the *ferrade*. The men fetch out a young bullock a year or two old, and drive him over to the fire. He is thrown down, and branded with a hot iron with the special mark of the farm he belongs to.

The foals have to be branded too. At about a year, they are caught with the lasso, their hooves are tied, and they are branded. The lasso is not usually thrown; the noose is attached to a long stick and slipped over the head of the animal to be marked.

When working with the bulls, the herdsmen are always on horseback, but when dealing with the horses themselves, they are often as not on foot. They sometimes spend the entire day in the saddle, except perhaps for a short break for lunch—if, for instance, they have to find and bring back a bull that has got away from the herd, they may spend all day riding through reed-beds, in and out of mud and water, in a perpetual cloud of mosquitoes.

After work, the horses are unsaddled and smacked over the rump to send them back to the wild.

Today, the great pastures are fenced, but until quite recent times some of the herds were guarded 'by hand'— by herdsmen, that is, keeping watch over the animals from morning till night along the vast stretches of unenclosed marsh and grass. At night they were driven into pens. Nowadays, this is only practised with sheep.

Festivals are delightfully frequent in the Camargue, and they all give the men a chance to show off their superb horsemanship, in the arena for the *jeux de gardians*, or in the *abrivados* and *banditos*. For the *abrivados* the herdsmen have to bring a number of bulls from pasture into the ring, via a given route through various villages. They drive the bulls over the route in v-formation as far as possible, using their horses to hem them in and keep them in line.

The *bandito* comes at the end of the day. The bulls, let loose in the open ring, scatter and run, and the riders have to collect and drive them back to pasture again. Speed and agility are the first requirements for these sports.

Working with bulls and horses demands long experience, fine horsemanship, pluck and persistence. The unforeseen often happens, and rare is the herdsman who does not carry the scar of some nasty situation somewhere about him.

On St George's Day every year in Arles, by a tradition which dates back to 1512, the blessing of horses and herdsmen takes place after High Mass.

There are few places like the Camargue, where man can find himself, by looking at the natural world about him, instead of looking inwardly, and by listening to other living creatures, instead of to himself.

This book shows the world of the Camargue—as it is today, living and wild; and as it must remain, if our own lives are to keep any meaning. But how long can it last? How long before this is only an album of souvenirs, enshrining a world we have lost? It is up to us to keep this world alive.

2

5

8

14

16

18

22

23

31

D

H 35

B

A

F

E

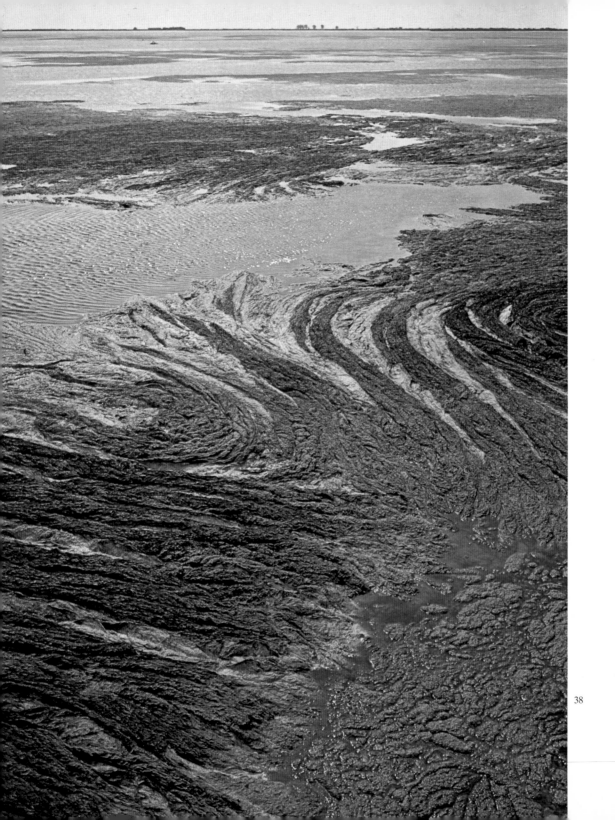

41

42

44

45

46

47

48

49

55

71

72